The Hats We Wear

Written and Illustrated by Robin L. Ham

Manufactured in the United States of America

Library of Congress Control Number: 2019918019
First Printing, 2020
ISBN: (Hardcover) 978-1-7337613-0-7
ISBN: (Paperback) 978-1-7337613-2-1
ISBN: (eBook) 978-1-7337613-1-4

Editor: Karla G. Jones

Front and back cover image design by Robin L. Ham
Illustrations, photography and graphic design by Robin L. Ham

Illustrations in this book are hand-rendered with color pencils, markers, and watercolor paints on multi-purpose paper.

The Hats We Wear

Written and Illustrated by Robin L. Ham

The front and back cover image of this book is the style of hat known as "Pillbox," with a birdcage veil (netting fabric) bow and brooch.

This hat is small, cylindrical in shape with straight sides, a flat crown top and no brim. Aristocratic women wore this style hat on the crown of the head during the 16th century. Pillbox hats were made from fur, leather, wool, velvet and silk, and often adorned with silk, netting, gold embroidery and pearls.

The netting fabric on the Pillbox style hat is also referred to as "tulle" and/or "mesh" if the fabric is knitted. The material is usually firm, lightweight and finely made with polyester, silk, nylon and rayon fibers. Tulle is also called "Birdcage Veil" because of its decorated netting style that covers the head and part of the face. The veil is sewn or glued to the hat and or attached with a comb to the hair.

During the Roman Empire, military soldiers wore hats emulating the pillbox-style, but with an attached chin-strap uniquely referred to as a "Pannonian Cap."

In the United States (North America), hotel attendants/bell hops or hotel porters (concierge or luggage check-in) wore similar version, known as Bellboy hats.

The hat reached prominence, however, in the early 1960s when First Lady, Jacqueline Kennedy was photographed at various occasions wearing pillbox-style hats designed by a milliner who later became a top American fashion designer known as Halston (real name Roy Halston Frowick). To this day, the hat remains very popular!

African American History:

Ann Lowe was the first African American dress designer for high-society socialites. Ann was commissioned by Joseph Kennedy Sr. in 1953 to design and construct Jacqueline Bouvier's bridal party dresses and her wedding gown when she married Senator John Fitzgerald Kennedy Jr., who later became the 35th President of the United States of America. In 1950, Ann opened "Ann Lowe's Gowns" in the village of Harlem, NY and in 1968, she opened "Ann Lowe's Originals" in Manhattan, New York's premier high-end retail shopping section on Madison Avenue. Ann became the first African American to own a retail store in this premier location.

Acknowledgments

Thank you, God, for bringing key people into my circle who have allowed me to experience and be exposed to all life has to offer, starting at a young age. As an adult I continue to appreciate the lessons I've learned along my journey through these individuals, many of whom rest in Heaven. I continue to grow from their words of wisdom.

Family and friends: Thank you for your support.

Joseph Ham (husband): You continuously teach me patience, hope, understanding, love and always reminds me to be grateful and thank God for all of my gifts and His mercy. You are my partner for life...

David I. Ellis (grandfather) aka "Granddaddy:" He helped me to understand and appreciate history, work ethics, integrity and honesty.

Mary E. Ellis (grandmother) aka "Granny:" She was a quiet-spirited woman who loved her family. I thank her for teaching me to have a kind heart, be empathetic and remember family values.

Dr. Delores E. Groves (mother): Because of you I have a spirit within that enables me to figure things out on my own, to keep a variety of friends, and to do what makes me happy and appreciate my many talents!

Clyde Groves (stepfather): Thank you for supporting my dreams...R.I.P.

Loretta Jones (grandmother, mother to Robert): To me she was like B.E. Smith and Martha Stewart wrapped up in one! I appreciated her more than she will ever know. She never bragged and was so very humble when it came to her own talents/gifts - and she had many. She will always remain the root of my creativity.

Robert L. Graves (father): He taught me the spirit of entrepreneurship and how to remain focused, even if it appeared all odds were against me. I thank God for blessing me with his multiple talents, inherited from him and his mother.

Diane Gary Bloodsaw: Thank you for being the best neighbor and family friend and always supporting me since seventh grade.

Sandranette Sellers: I thank you for proofreading my early copy of this book.

Karla Jones Penn: Thank you for your expertise service when it came to editing my final copy. You have been truly a gem who I appreciate on this journey.

The Greater Hudson Valley (NY) Chapter of the Links, Incorporated (GHVNY), and members – Thank you for trusting in me and giving me the opportunity to create and design whenever needed. There's one particular project that comes to mind: Butterfly Medicine©, a Domestic Violence Campaign. This project allowed me to tap back into my creative side and focus on completing this book.

Coincidentally, the hat design on the cover of this book was inspired by a GHV (NY) Links, Incorporated Chapter member. She wore it at an annual "Ladies In Hats" fundraising luncheon.

FOREWORD

"It takes a village to raise a child." I am deeply honored to have been a loving and nurturing part of the village of Robin L. Ham. I proudly embraced the titles of neighbor and family friend, along with other proxy parents to the myriad of youth who lived on our street in Shaker Heights, Ohio. During her youth, most of the young people entertained themselves in activities that enthusiastically required running, riding, and rolling - be it on foot, skates, bicycles or boards, on our otherwise quiet residential street. In distinct contrast to the zealous fun and games of these children, Robin -, modestly and purposefully - created her own inspirational atmosphere at home, or in libraries and museums She thrived in places that provided her the atmosphere to individualize her persona by devoting and cultivating her attention to creating, developing and exhibiting her creative talents. Her activities of choice included sporting games with friends and family, reading fashion magazines, creating and drawing in sketch pads or honing her photographic skills. As a middle-schooler, at the top of Robin's "Christmas Wish List" was a sewing machine. Devoted to her purpose, her dreams began to materialize during these early teen years as she participated and excelled in events that exhibited her amazing art and creative talents. Fashions she designed were often featured in local fashion shows, not to mention she produced several events that showcased her beautiful designs! To this day, I continue to wear a dress she crafted for me over 25 years ago. It's a classic, timeless piece.

Devoted to her purpose, Robin continued her quest through education at The Fashion Institute of Technology in New York City, N.Y. and an adventurous sojourn to Paris, France, where she broadened her horizons by enhancing her skills and experiences. Robin's devotion to her family, friends, and the world of business and management and worthy causes remains constant, confident and courageous priorities in her life. William Shakespeare's quote is most fitting of our author, Robin L. Ham as she continues to exemplify, "This Above All, To Thine Own Self Be True."

I was delighted to receive the exciting news that Robin authored this wonderful book, "The Hats We Wear"! It is fitting and timely in the path of her journey. She delves into research and provides a unique literary expression of a subject that is interesting, compelling, and creative. The reader is about to embark on a fascinating journey... Creativity meets history and knowledge. Hats are universal, found in all walks of life, for all ages, a variety of uses, designed in an array of styles, both contemporary and traditional. Hats are symbolic and hats have stories. I invite the reader to enjoy their journey of enlightenment into Hats!

- Diane Gary Bloodsaw

*It Takes a Village to Raise a Child" is an African proverb that means an entire community of people must interact with children for those children to experience and grow in a safe and healthy environment. The villagers look out for the children. Wikipedia

Author's Note

The sole purpose of this book is to educate and spark an interest (especially in the children of our next generation) about the history behind hats and head dressings. I want to encourage a spirit of being openminded to the differences we may have without feeling the need to ridicule one another. As it stands, hats have been both an object of ridicule as well as beauty. This book only touches on commonly-worn hats and scarves. To this current day, there are thousands of hat styles and head dressings. As such, many are not represented in this book.

Why hats? I've recently reflected on how hats have played an important part of my life. As a native of Louisville, Kentucky, I began life literally with a bonnet on my head at birth. Growing up, hats were everywhere – worn by men, women and children. As a child, my sister, Angela Graves Payden and I always wore stylish and practical hats, scarves or big ribbons and bows...

My grandmother, Mary Ellis, loved to shop and purchase beautiful clothes and hats; a tradition she passed onto my mother (Dr. Delores E. Groves), who then passed it on to my sister Angela and me.

My grandfather, David Ellis, was a photographer at heart and hobby. He was always taking pictures and creating scrapbooks of his clippings of sporting and current event newspaper articles. These books are still in our family today! My sister and I would enjoy looking at his pictures and scrapbooks while he shared wonderful family stories and history. Listening to those stories and looking at the clothes and hats was exciting and fascinating.

As an adult, living in New York and traveling abroad has afforded me the opportunity to meet people from around the world who have different religious beliefs and lifestyles that they manifest through headwear. These experiences have helped me develop an appreciation for unique independence, while building upon my love for hats. I proudly embrace and endorse this tradition borne within my family.

This is a multi-cultural illustrated book for adults and children. It chronicles some of my experiences as a child and as an adult. It is intended for any person interested in diverse cultures, history, values, the religious meaning of hats and the beauty of hats illustrated in a fun way. My hope for this book is to provoke discussion about respecting people's differences. It's a way to reflect, reminisce and hold on to a beautiful tradition that has been in existence since the beginning of time.

Introduction

For centuries, people have worn hats for duty, protection and fashion. Royalty, noblemen, military, warriors, athletes, religious leaders, pharaohs, laborers, and peasants – the list is endless. Hats have been documented since 2000 BC with their assortment of fabrications, including various leaves, feathers, fur, fabrics, grosgrain ribbons, novelty trims, felts, straw, metals, precious stones and more. These materials were used to construct, style and decorate hats, crowns and headdresses. History always repeats itself, and styles from the past are relevant today.

This book touches on some of the history and traditions of hats and headdresses from various cultures, as well as the people who wear them. The intent is to help eliminate prejudice and misconceptions about people, their lifestyles and beliefs. Understanding the cultural differences around the world and why hats and headdresses are important will help others respect the global traditions and beliefs that exist.

Consequently, this is not a book about how to wear hats per se, it's a book about people and their faith(s), honor, purpose, protection, understanding and tolerance, feeling good about oneself, confidence, (and if you choose) just making a fashion statement.

Instructions for Story Teller:

When reading from this book (if time and budget allows) it would be awesome if the presenter/storyteller were to wear or have a display of hats shown ("show & tell") as an artistic expression and to provoke a healthy dialogue. After all, what is more precious than seeing a child (or even an adult) willingly engaged in the excitement of learning and being a part of the moment of storytelling?

Hint: You can take this idea one step further by asking your audience ahead of time to bring in hats they own that represent their cultural experiences.

Millinery "Hat" Shop

Wow! So many hats in Mrs. Theodore's Store … can't wait to step through the door.

History:
A Milliner is a person who makes and creates hats, and millinery is the practice of selling hats and headwear for women and men to accessorize their wardrobe. During the 15th century, Milan, Italy was known for beautiful fabrics, clothes, ribbons, bonnets and goods. Hence, the name millinery was coined in the 1700s from Milan, Italy. It means "A shop of hats." Milliners were required to provide high levels of service by understanding the customer's social life and keeping up with the latest fashions using the stylish materials, novelty trims and ribbons.

Lock & Co. Hatters is the oldest, family-owned hat shop in the world. Established in 1676, the shop is located on 6 St James's Street, London, England. This shop is sought out because of its reputation for service and quality, and as such serves royalty, political figures, celebrities and more. Among its most famous hats, Lock & Co. created a rounded firm crown hat with a short shaped upturned brim in 1849 called the Bowler Hat (Coke Hat).

Pom-poms

Tasty snowflakes fall from the sky, as I wear my knitted pompom hat to keep me warm and dry.

History:

Pom-poms date back to the Vikings from 800 to 1066 in Scandinavia. It was said that the name originated from the French word "pompom" (a small decorative ball made of yarn, fabric or feathers) or "ornamental round tuft," during the 18th century. Other cultures also used pom-pom on hats for uniforms and traditional garments for men and women, such as in South America, Scotland (Tam-o'-Shanter or Toorie bonnet and Balmoral bonnet worn by men), Napoleon's army and Clergymen in Rome ("Birettlas" square-peaked caps with a pom-pom).

Ushanka means, "ear hat" in Russian. In English, it is called "Chapka" or "Russian hat." During the 17th century, northern and central Russia wore this hat for warmth; at that time, it was called "treukh." Similar hats existed before the 17th century in Balkan, Scandinavia, Ukraine, Russia and Northern Italy. The Ushanka is usually made with sheepskin, rabbit and sometimes fox fur with earflaps fastening under the chin with a snap or tie.

The least expensive version of this hat is made with wool pile, cloth or leather and artificial fur also called "fish fur" or "faux fur." The design of this hat showcases a round crown, fold down visor and earflaps (usually with strings to tie under the chin or on top of the head). Similar hats existed before the 17th century in Balkan, Scandinavia, Ukraine and Russia.

* The Snowman is wearing a soft short brim hat round crown Fedora.

Rain Hats

As I wear my hat in the rain, the water hits it, beads up and washes away...

History:
Amazonian Indians were the first known to extract a milky substance from rubber trees, which was then called "rubber," to waterproof their clothing during the 13th century. By 1748, Francois Fresneau was a French botanist scientist credited for his writings on waterproofing materials using rubber. James Syme, a chemist of Scotland furthered Fresneau's research and subsequently invented a waterproof cloth in 1821, Syme ended his research and later became a renowned surgeon.

Scottish inventor and chemist Charles Macintosh combined rubber and plastic, discovering that these two materials can create waterproof fabric. While many others created similar products, Macintosh was the first to patent his waterproof coat in 1823 and was credited for creating waterproof raincoats.

Around 1900, the bucket or fishing hat was introduced. This hat is fitted on the crown of the head with a brim slightly covering the face and around the head to protect from the rain. Irish farmers and fisherman wore the original hats. Natural fabrics were used such as wool felt and tweed cloth because of the warmth, durability and water-repellent nature. Unwashed raw wool was great to use because the lanolin creates a water repellent. Today, many rain hats are made with waterproof nylon fabrics, cotton, terry cloth, wool and more for protection and style.

"Sou'wester" is another waterproof hat style. It contains a wide, slanting short brim in front and longer brim in the back used by many fishermen.

Cowboy Hats

Ride'm Cowgirl is a phrase I use, when I put on my western hat, shirt and boots. Time to saddle up...

History:
Cowboy traditions stem from medieval Spain because of the style of cattle ranching practiced there that was later adopted by other cultures. Spaniards and Mexican Vaqueros have worn Sombrero hats since the 13th century as horseback riders; they called themselves Mongolian Horseman in Central Mexico. The people of the Philippines were also influenced by the sombrero hat style as trade grew during 1565 to 1815. Sombreros were ideal for the outdoor lifestyle of the cowboy. Their design includes a broad-brim for optimal shade and a high crown to also assist with coolness; these hats were worn for work and casual occasions.

Working American cowboys wore high-crowned hats that were influenced by the "10 gallon" style (hatbands braided and attached to a large crown sombrero). The cowboys later changed the name to "gallon" and started calling their hat style Ten-Gallon Hats.

In the 1860s, cowboy hats took over the Western United States with a heavy style influence from the sombrero. A U.S. hat maker, John B. Stetson, modernized the "cowboy hat" and created the "Stetson," known to many and referenced today as the modern-day "Cowboy Hat." It came in one style: flat "waterproof" brimmed, straight sided 4" crown with rounded corners, natural in color and made into felt with fine fur from beavers, rabbits and other small animals finishing the design with a plain fitted hatband.

Bonnets

As I wear my "Bonnet" … Blowing bubbles on Grandma's front porch is fun to do with just us two!

History:
Bonnets originated from Scotland in 1505 during the Middle Ages. Bonnets are head coverings made of soft materials with or without a front brim worn on top or on back of the head usually with a tie under the chin. As hats and hoods were so popular during the Middle Ages, it is believed bonnets were a variation based on those styles.

Materials used for bonnets included straw, silk and other fabrics. Examples include:

- Lacy lingerie caps "Capote" (soft bonnets with a stiff brim) (1700)
- Baby bonnets provided warmth to infants and toddlers (1812)
- Brims expanded with the elaborate hairstyles and fashions using bows, plumes, ribbons and various flowers (1820) and
- Hanging ribbon streams with no chin ties (1830).

Various styles of bonnets have been popular through the years such as: poke and bibi, bonnet sleep cap and more. The Quakers, Old Order Mennonites and Amish women continue to wear bonnets in the 21st century.

Sun Hats

On any breezy and sunny day, my Granny and I would hang clothes outdoors to dry.

Working Hats

History:
Approximately 3200 B.C., one of the first pictorial depictions of a woven style hat (conical) appears in a tomb painting from Thebes, Egypt. It was said that the upper class Egyptians shaved their head and used a "headdress covering" to keep cool.

Sunbonnets and straw hats come in several styles. The purpose of these hats is to provide shade by protecting the face from the sun while working in the field's and/or everyday yard work, outdoor activities and also as a fashion statement. Some hats are handmade, others with machines, plaited or woven. There are several materials used, including:

- Palm Leaves
- Plant Fibers
- Sea Grass
- Bamboo
- Rush, Wheat and Hemp Straw.

The Cone or Rice hat below is a globally-styled hat mainly used throughout Asia as a working hat. In Thailand it is called "Kramon Ngob" and in Vietnam its called "Conical." Straps are used to secure the hat to the head.

Floppy Beach Hat

My big sister wears her floppy beach hat that protects her skin from the sun, while I'm in the sand having fun...

The floppy hat is a wide brim hat used for shading the face and shoulders from the sun. These colorful, fun hats are often decorated with flowers, ribbons, beads and more.

History:

During the fourteenth century, peasants wore this style for protection from the sun. Over time, this hat became stylish and was used for several purposes.

"Seaside" hats were popularized during the 18th century as people began enjoying the sea and beaches. Straw hats have usually been made the same way for peasants to the elite. These hats have been considered a symbol of freedom and life outdoors while protecting the skin from the sun's rays.

Swim Caps

We wear our swim caps while sitting by the pool, enjoying the display of fun hat colors; textures and styles that make us look cool!

History:
Bathing or swim caps were created during the 19th century. The original material for bathing or swim caps was natural rubber or rubberized waterproof fabric. Later other synthetic materials were used, such as Latex and Lycra©, for their stretch capability and their ability to prevent the hair from getting wet. In the 1920s, the "Aviator" style swim cap was introduced. This style offered a snap from ear to ear underneath the chin imitating a pilot's hat.

These hats became fun and stylish with various colors, bows, flowers, tassels, attached curled nylon hair, pearls, textures, puffy turbans and much more. Often these hats were woven and worn as outerwear (with cloths as accessories).

8 FEET

CHURCHILL DOWNS

**FIRST DERBY
1875**

Riding Hats

Horses circle the track, (Hippity-Hop) or hip-hip hooray! Every first Saturday in May is Kentucky Derby Day!

Kentucky Derby History:
The Run for the Roses is a special day filled with fun in Louisville, Kentucky. The first Kentucky Derby was in 1875 at which time the race distance was a 1.5-mile race at Churchill Downs track. Today the distance is 1.25 miles.

The Derby was traditionally known for its style. Women dressed up as Southern Belles with beautifully and creatively decorated hats, and many were quite over-the-top hats and flamboyant outfits embellished with bows, ribbons, flowers, jewels, feathers and more. Men and children also dressed up in bright color clothes and hats to cheer on the jockeys and their horses.

Riding Hats History:
There are several riding hats. Equestrian Helmets or Rider Caps also called Skull Caps date back to around 750 - 800 B.C. to the ancient Roman Mediterranean Charioteers (Chariot Drivers or Racers). The charioteers wore this protective headgear, which was made of forged bronze formed by heating and hammering it into shape or leather helm or a wide leather belt comprised of many straps and shaped to fit the head with a visor.

Teams represented by Factions (backers) were identified/named-using colors. Each color had a meaning such as: Red (summer), Blue (sky, sea and Autumn), White (winter), and Green (spring). The colors were used to keep track of races.

In England, the British covered riding helmets in velvet with a peak or visor and hatbands fastened at the front with a buckle. The British National Jockey Club established the rules and regulations for the sport in 1880, requiring horse owners register colors for their jockey caps and rider's shirts. This ruling helps spectators identify jockeys and horses during races.

Helmets made in the 21st century are constructed with a hard-outer shell of a fiberglass or composite fiber, polycarbonate, carbon fiber or Kevlar (Expanded Polystyrene Styrofoam™ called (EPS) foam, made to conform to the head; with a Styrofoam™ for the inner lining.

KENTUCKY DERBY

It is vented for coolness; lacing to cradle the back of the head harness system for stability and a fastening chin strap and a bib or brim to provide shade. They are designed to protect the entire head as falls often occur. This helmet or headgear is constantly tested and improving to meet the American Society for Testing and Materials (ASTM) and Safety Equipment Institute (SEI) performance safety standards.

Jockeys today wear oversized cap covers and jackets in vibrant colors representing stables and owners similar to the chariot riders in Ancient Rome. The fabrics used for cap covers are made of silk, nylon, satin and Lycra®.

African American History:

African American jockeys dominated horse racing after the Civil War, (winning 15 of the first 28 Kentucky Derby races). During this time many of these jockeys were slaves working the stables as riders, groomers, and trainers. Here are a few names of exemplary people of color (who because of "race") had a limited career in the horse racing industry.

Oliver Lewis (1856-1924) was the first professional African American jockey, who won an amazing three Kentucky Derby races. Ansel Williamson (a former slave) trained Mr. Lewis' horse ("Aristides"). After the emancipation, Ansel Williamson trained another winning horse by the name of "Baden-Baden", its rider was none other than Ed Brown. Brown won the 1877 Kentucky Derby. Williamson parlayed his success and eventually opened and operated his own racing stable.

Isaac Burns Murphy (the first jockey to win successive Derby crowns) was inducted into the National Museum of Racing and Hall of Fame (created in 1955). He rode the horse, "Kingman", a thoroughbred owned by a former slave Dudley Allen, who was the first and only African American man to own a horse that won the Kentucky Derby.

Willie Simms was the only African American jockey to win The Big Three races (known as the *Triple Crown*) the *Kentucky Derby*, the *Preakness* and the *Belmont Stakes*. Simms was an inductee in the U.S. Racing Hall of Fame.

In 1902, as Jim Crow laws swept through Kentucky, many horse owners temporarily removed African American jockeys. During the early 19th century in New York State, white jockeys campaigned by threatening trainers and owners by demanding they avoid mounting black riders or suffer the consequences. These white riders would sabotage races by "boxing" the black jockeys into and often, over the railings. It wasn't until the year of (1911) that black jockey Jimmy Winkfield was allowed to race in the Kentucky Derby.

Church Hats

As they wear their hats, ladies come to church all dressed looking their best, with hats on their heads fit for a celebrity guest.

African American History:
Slave owners did not care for the texture or look of their slave's hair, especially those who worked in their homes. In fact, many slave owners required their slaves to cover their heads while working.

As a result, Sundays were the only day of the week fancy hats could be worn since slaves worked a minimum of six days a week. For slaves, wearing hats on Sunday was an expression of creativity and style, as well as to look pretty. Slaves would embellish their field hats with flowers, ribbons and fabrics to create different-shaped hats of various colors, shapes and sizes. Also, wearing hats gave slaves a sense of confidence and inspiration, as they honored and respected "God" by covering their heads during worship, a practice originating from the Biblical scripture (1 Corinthians 11:5), "But every woman that prayeth or prophesieth with her head uncovered dishonoureth her head…"This tradition is still practiced in African American churches.

Africa

As they wear their hats, headdresses and scarves across the continent of rich and beautiful Africa from the North, South, East and West, with vibrant colors, beads, fabrics and more I do adore.

History:

The diverse continent of Africa has over 3,000 ethnic groups who speak more than 2,100 different languages or dialects. It's only natural this wide cultural range also spans an equally wide range of hat styles and headwear dating back to antiquity. Hats were worn for ceremonies, festivals, war, working in the hot sun and common daily living. Some of these hats were elaborate and were often associated with one's social and political status, including royalty, tribal kings, queens, chiefs, Nobles and elders. Crowns, diadems, caps, hats, headdress and head wraps offer a variety of functions and use among each culture. Often hats, head dressings, scarves (hijab), wrapped turbans and long robes provided protection from the sun, heat, wind-blown sand, rain and cold. Turbans and Hijab's also have significant religious meaning in the Islamic religion beginning in the 17th century.

Imagination, creativity and precision embody the continent of Africa. Many useful items have been created in Africa such as: furniture, paints, certain hats, engineering and much more. Hats and head dressings were and still are constructed with the following items: jute, banana leaves, glass, iron beads, cowrie shells, buttons, wood, feathers, plumes, mussel shells, teeth, seed pods, tusks, elephant tails, string, gourds, vegetable fibers and horn bill, burlap, grass, cotton, sheep and goat hair, precious stones, felt, fur, and animal skins from crocodiles, goats, leopards and other creatures.

African American History:

In 1831 "A Muslim American Slave, The Life of Omar ibn Said" was published. It chronicled the life of Omar ibn Said, who was a wealthy man, an educated writer and an Islamic scholar from Futa Tooro, Senegal, West Africa. At the age of 37 in 1807, he was abducted, enslaved, sold and transported to Charleston, South Carolina (USA) by slave traders.

Omar was the only known Muslin slave who documented his slavery journey. After he escaped the plantation and was jailed soon after, he began writing his journal on the jail walls in Arabic (not knowing English). His writings caught the attention of Governor James Owens of North Carolina, and Omar was released from the jail. At the age of 60 and still a slave, Omar wrote his book in his Arabic language so it would be in his own words unaltered. Omar ibn Said is wearing a cloth headwrap in the above photograph.

Native American

Respecting Mother Earth is a necessity; our bodies are rooted in the earth just like nature...

History:

The indigenous people (native or first peoples) of America are known as Native Americans, American Indians and Indigenous Americans. They wore colorful headdress made with feathers, beads and animal skins worn during religious ceremonies, intimidating enemies during battle, protection from inclement weather, etc. While movies and photographs show Native Americans wearing large feathered war bonnets, these were seldom worn in battle due to their construction, size and practicality from a comfort standpoint. Each feather in a war bonnet indicated an act of bravery:

- Trailer war bonnet – an extension of feathers down the warrior's back usually in one or two rows
- Halo war bonnet – feathers circling around the face
- Straight-up feather war bonnet – tall and narrow feathers sticking upward and
- The Roach headdress (porcupine roach) – worn by North American Indians; Mohawk, Pawnee, Huron, Sauk, Fox, Osage, and Pequot.

African American History:

Bass Reeves (1838-1910) was born into slavery in Arkansas and grew up in Grayson County, Texas. The Reeves family, under whom he became an excellent marksman, owned him. After a fight with the family, Reeves fled to Indian Territory (known today as Kansas and Oklahoma).

After an extended period of time in Indian Territory, Reeves served in several battles. He built relationships with many Indian tribes, knew the terrain, learned the culture and language and eventually become an asset to the U.S. government by working as a guide for the U.S. government, traveling through Indian Territory. In 1875, U.S. Federal Judge Isaac Parker of the Western District of Arkansas commissioned him to be the First Black U.S. Marshal. While other marshals protested, Reeves' strong marksman skills, physical presence (6'2"), fluency with several Indian languages, keen memory and overall ambidexterity solidified the appointment.

His responsibilities were to police and manage 75,000 square miles of Oklahoma and Arkansas with other Marshals. Arkansas records credit him with killing 14 outlaws and apprehending over 3,000 others (including his son Bennie Reeves).

Reeves retired in 1907 and became a police officer in Muskogee, Oklahoma. Thanks to his well-respected and legendary status, speculation has been that Bass Reeves was the fictional character "Lone Ranger."

Orthodox and Hasidic Jewish Men

Black suits and white shirts with no gray, as we start our day to Pray!

History:

The Homburg is an oval shape crown hat with a brim (pencil curl around edge), made of stiff wool felt with a center crease "gutter crown" on top and usually has a grosgrain ribbon band.

The name Homburg originated from the word Bad Homburg from the Hesse, Germany Empire. King Edward VII of the United Kingdom of Great Britain also wore this hat; it was originally used as hunting head-gear. During the 19th century, it became popular when worn by UK Prime Minister Winston Churchill as his signature hat. Dwight D. Eisenhower (34th President of the United States of America) wore a black homburg, as well, during his 1953 inauguration.

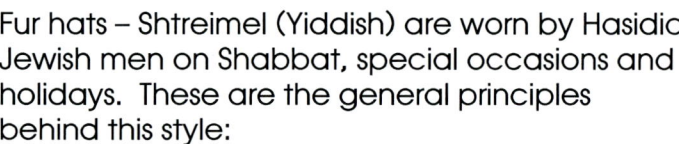

There are several styles of the rounded crown (oval shape) fedoras.

Fur hats – Shtreimel (Yiddish) are worn by Hasidic Jewish men on Shabbat, special occasions and holidays. These are the general principles behind this style:

- Made of genuine fur from the tails of Canadian or Russian sable, stone marten, baum marten or American gray fox also synthetic fur (common in Israel)
- Worn after marriage, the bride's father is responsible for buying it for the groom
- Some have two, one less expensive (rain shtreimel) worn during inclement weather and the more expensive version for special occasions and
- For additional spiritual value the kippah is always worn underneath the shtreimel (custom not a law).

Non-Orthodox Jews may not wear the kippah while out every day. They may only wear it during prayer service and special occasions and holidays:

- Kippah – in Hebrew it means (skull cap); in Yiddish it means Yarmelke
- Satin – conservative and reform
- Black velvet – Haredi Orthodox
- Crocheted – Israel's religious Zionists
- Suede – modern Orthodox and
- Bukharan – Sephardic and central Asian Jews.

Pope - Skullcap

As an act of kindness, reach out to others in need as a good deed.

History:
Zucchetto (commonly referred to as a skullcap) may have been created during the 15th century; it is also known as pilus, pilos, pileus, pileolus, subbiretum, submtrale, soli deo, berret-tino and calotte. The skullcap is form-fitting and made with silk or polyester fabric worn on the crown of the head. The difference between the zucchetto and the Jewish kippah is the fabrication, size of panels and stem in the center. The construction for the zucchetto is as follows: cut in 8 triangular panels forming a skullcap, thin leather liner for insulation and shape; a strip of velvet to secure the fit, cloth lining and a "stem" at the center top is a twisted loop of silk cord called "stirpes" (used to handle the zucchetto easier). This hat is never worn with a suit.

Roman Catholic clerics, Syriac Orthodox Church and high clergy in Anglicanism wear the zucchetto. There are different colors based on the hierarchy such as:

- White – The Pope
- Bright Red/ Scarlet - Cardinal
- Warm Reddish Rose - Archbishops, Bishop, territorial, abbots and territorial prelates and
- Black - Priest and Deacons.

Arab Men

Covering our head helps protect us from the extreme heat and sandstorms while staying cool...

History:

Modest dressing and decency are important to the Islamic community. The ghutrah (ghatar) is a square cloth (plain white or checkered and sometimes embroidered) worn as a headdress by Arab men. The ghutrah is a lightweight cotton scarf square folded diagonally into a triangle, with the fold placed across the forehead and the fabric draped over the head with the ends down the back and shoulders. Once placed on the head, it is held on with a strong cord (agal, egal or igal), usually made of goat hair. This is worn doubled to keep the ghutrah in place.

Men from countries in the Gulf such as Saudi Arabia, Kuwait, Bahrain, Qatar, the United Arab Emirates and Oman wear Ghutra, Kafiya and Keffiyeh or Shemagh headdresses.

The Ghutrah has been worn for over 200 years along with the "dishdasha" (a long white robe usually worn by men in the Middle East). Dishdashas help protect from the desert's severe heat, wind and sandstorms. They also demonstrate nationality, status and religion.

It was said that the Prophet Muhammad taught that protection from misguided problems would come if one covered the head. The men in the United Arab Emirates wore head cloths in dimensions ranging from 42 square inches up to 52 square inches (increasing by 2-inch increments all around).

Sikhism

We neatly secure and cover our uncut hair to honor and praise those before us who showed us how we should care...

History:
During the 15th century in Northern India, Guru Nanak Dev "Baba Nanak" founded the Sikh faith. The Sikh's are NOT Muslim; they have a different religion and set of beliefs.

The origin of the turban is uncertain; some say Persia (Iran), and others say Egyptians were the inventors. The Dastar (turban) means "the hand of God" and is worn by Sikh's. Wearing the dastar symbolizes spirituality, obedience, humility, honor and respect for the founder. One of the articles of faith is for men and women to cover their unshorn (uncut) hair in public places.

At the age of two, boys begin wearing a topknot that is usually covered with a cotton or nylon patka (starter turban) and is not wrapped around the head. The topknot is placed over the hairline, with the two front ends tied in the back, and the back ends tied around the hair creating a bun on top. Once they reach ages 7 to 14, a special coming-of-age ceremonial is given called the dastar bandhi where he puts on his first pagri (turban). This turban is for ceremonial purposes only, and once complete, the boy will go back wearing the patka. It is important that young Sikh boys learn how to properly wrap their headdress and become used to the weight. Most start wearing turbans full-time once they reach their late teens.

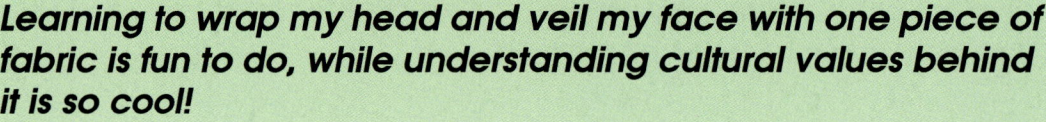

Head Scarves

Learning to wrap my head and veil my face with one piece of fabric is fun to do, while understanding cultural values behind it is so cool!

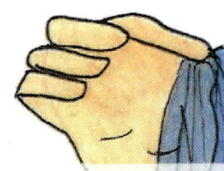

History:

Men and women for various reasons wear scarves such as: religion, culture, protection from the sun, mourning a loss, customs, hair loss, illness and style. Scarves are the most flexible head covering to wear.

Usually European peasant women, ethnically dressed, wore scarves or kerchiefs with bold colors and detailed designs made of cottons, silks and other fabrics. Scarves were also worn during feast days and holidays, for practicality and fashion.

Tichel (tickle) Scarf

When a Hasidic or Orthodox Jewish woman marries, she covers her head in public with a wig, hat or scarf called a tichel (depending on her community). Once she is in her home, she may remove the covering.

Married Jewish women may wear a scarf with three corners called Mitpachat in (Hebrew) or Tichel in (Yiddish) - both terms mean Kerchief and or Scarf. Liberal reformed Jewish women do not wear such head coverings.

It is said that a passage in the Torah speaks on one occasion about a woman's infidelity in her marriage with another man. This case was tried in the Jewish courts and the woman was required to remove her head covering, considered the greatest shame and causing humiliation, along with changing the woman's status in her culture.

Overall, scarves became fashionable and popularized in the 1960s when worn by Jacqueline Kennedy, First Lady of the United States.

Other cultures that wear headscarves include: Indian, Muslim, African, Native American, Japanese, Turks, Eastern Europeans, Bangladeshis, Jewish Orthodox, Sikhs, African American, Spanish Catholic Orthodox Church, Islam, Ethiopian Orthodox Church and Hindu.

Dupetta and Adhivasa

Dupetta is a head covering worn in India. It differs from a Hijab or a stole or shawl by being 2 to 3 yards longer and worn to cover the head in the presence of elders and in the place of worship by Hindu families.

The Adhivasa is similar to a Dupatta and is worn by the Vedic India people and the Chador is worn in Pakistan.

Veil's

Veils have been in existence for over 4,000 years. From early times to the present day, the veil remains the most versatile and exclusive headwear for women. Certain religions require a woman to have their heads and hair covered in public. The practice of veiling is a law in some cultures, and it also may indicate the women's marital status and social standing.

The Niqab (meaning "to perforate") is a veil draped over or around the face with two holes or slits that expose only the woman's eyes. The practice of wearing niqabs possibly dates back to the beginning of Islam. Areas known for wearing them include Saudi Arabia and several North African countries including Algeria and Morocco.

Chador (meaning "large cloth" or "sheet" in Persian) – is a semicircular cloak, usually black in color that is draped around the women's head and body with the face typically exposed. This style dates back to the Abbasid era (750-1258) in Persia, and is worn outdoors in modern Iran and sometimes in other Central Asian countries.

Women from Kabul use the term Tradit "Chadri" or the "Burqa," which fully covers the head, face and body with an embroidered mesh vent so the wearer can visually see and be able to breathe. In Afghanistan and parts of Pakistan, as well as India, some garments are considered controversial, so they are not allowed to be worn in public. Therefore, some head and clothing styles suggest the wearer balance the value of individual rights and religious freedom versus public safety.

Hijab (Arabic for Hajaba): means to conceal or hide from view. Islamic women for centuries have worn this religious veiling as part of the practice of covering their hair and bodies as a sign of modesty and commitment to the teaching of the Prophet Muhammad.

The Girl Scouts of the USA Hat

Always a Girl Scout camping, meeting new people and learning a ton, while following my big sister around just for fun!

History:

In 1912, Juliette Gordon Low nicknamed, "Daisy," founded a girl's youth group called Girl Scouts of the United States of America (GSUSA), commonly referred to as Girl Scouts. Juliette was 51 years old, living in her hometown of Savannah, Georgia. She was also nearly deaf, but she had a vision of preparing girls to develop lifelong friendships and to embrace their world with courage, confidence, self-worth and character.

One component of the Girl Scouts uniform is the hat. Depending on the girl's level, which is based on her age and experience, she is required to wear specific uniforms and accessories. Throughout the years, the uniforms and hats have changed. My sister and I actually were Girl Scouts in the late 60s and 70s. Here are some of the many hat styles:

- Girl Scout Brownie – Brown rounded felt Beanie or Skull Cap
- Girl Scout Juniors – Dark Green wool Beret*
- Girl Scout Cadette – Green felt Beret
- Girl Scout Senior – Bright Green Beret made of cotton gabardine that matches the dress uniform and
- Girl Scout Adult Uniform – Green Beret, fabric 65% Dacron® and 35% rayon.

* A Beret is a round, flat-crowned style hat with a center stem.

African American History:

In 1917, one of the earliest African American GSUSA troops was formed, followed in 1921 with a Native American GSUSA troop and in the 1930s, a Mexican American troop.

By the 1950s, a national effort was made by the GSUSA to desegregate. Select Girl Scouts in the United States and some guest from foreign countries were invited to attend the Girl Scout Senior Roundup. The Roundup was held June 29 to July 10, 1956 at High State Park in Milford, Michigan. They gathered to show off the best in Girl Scouting. My mother, Dr. Delores E. Groves, participated in this historic event with one of her childhood friends. They were the only two African Americans selected from troops in Louisville, Kentucky to attend.

From 1969 to 1972, an African American named Dr. Dorothy B. Ferebee served as the fourth Vice President of GSUSA. From 1975 to 1978, Dr. Gloria Randle Scott was the first African American National President of GSUSA.

Pastry Hat

The aroma of fresh baked goods in the air and plenty to share!

History:

The tam-o'-shanter chef hat served two important functions; (1) To safely carry trays of pastries and bread on the head and (2) protect the skull from the heat.

Marie-Antoine Carême was a French-born chef born in 1784-1883. He was credited with creating the standard "Chefs Hat." Carême is one of the first renowned (what we now refer to as) a Celebrity Chef.

To avoid losing the importance of the floppy Tam-O'-Shanter Chefs Hat, Carême decided to change the design. He noticed a girl on the street in Vienna wearing a stiff white cap and copied the idea by stiffening a traditional high cap with a circlet of cardboard. This design became popular throughout Europe and North America making it a very popular fashion called "Toque," which is still used today.

The "Toque blanche" (*French for "white hat") is a starched tall white pleated hat with a short round brim; chefs throughout centuries have worn this hat. The height of toque may indicate the chefs rank within a kitchen. The number of pleats indicate how many techniques or recipes the chefs have mastered cooking eggs (the magic number is 101 ways to cook an egg).

Hairnets:

Hairnets are one of the oldest forms of human headwear, dating back to around 22,000 BCE (likely from plant fibers). A "Hairnet," "Net," or "Caul" head covering is used to contain the hair. It is constructed to be a flexible, stretch mesh screen or netting produced from several materials including natural fibers, silken threads, human or animal hair, modern synthetics, chenille, cord, and ribbon. Hairnets have been worn for fashion, workplace environment safety, ritual objects and sanitary reasons while preparing and serving food.

African American History: (freed slaves)

- Mrs. Malinda Russell, published in 1866, one of the first African American Women's, "Domestic Cook Book" (29 page pamphlet) and

- Abby Fisher published in 1881, "What Mrs. Fisher Knows About Old Southern Cooking." She won medals and prizes for best pickles, sauces, jellies and preserves and also for her great culinary skills.

Birthday Party Hats

As I wear my colorful pointed "Cone Shaped Hat" w/sparkles, glitter and fluffs ready to celebrate my special day blowing out my candle with one big puff!

History:

The Cone/Cylindrical hat is said to have originated from Egypt around 2800 B.C. This style was worn by nobility and passed down from pharaoh to pharaoh (no one-specific origin has been noted). There were many designs to help identify a pharaoh. The style was worn to show distinction and as a symbol of power and/or status.

Europe in the 15th century developed medieval cone-shaped hats worn by princesses and inspired by Mongol warrior women, Catholic princesses, and noble women in medieval Europe. These hats were often decorated with lace, veils flowers, etc. Other religions and cultures began wearing cone or cylindrical hats called "Sugar-Loaf Hat." This shape also cooled the head by trapping air inside the cone.

The "Dunce-Cap" as its typically known is used for misbehavior and punishment. By the mid-19th to 20th century, it was adopted as the "Birthday Hat," made of cardboard and decorated with colors, sparkles, fuzzy fur and more, and worn to celebrate that special day and/or worn with Halloween costumes as a princes hat.

Hoods

Hoods and hoodies are the same; keeping warm and stylish is my game!

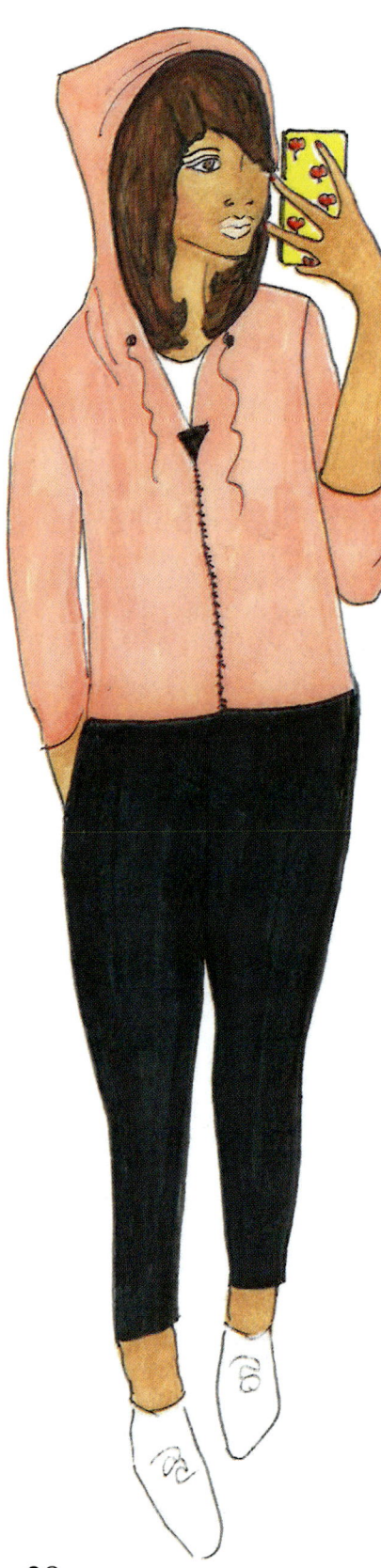

History:
Hoods date back thousands of years (ca. 25,000 B.C.) with discoveries at prehistoric burial sites.

Men and women from around the world have worn hooded garments for protection from the inclement weather, costumes, ceremonial costumes, status and style.

In the 1960s and 70s hoods on athletic wear became popular among students, who use them as casual wear. Later, the popularity grew as pop culture icons and rap and hip-hop artists started wearing these sweatshirts known as a *"Hoodie."* Minus its negative connotation, hoods are a very practical way of providing warmth and keeping up with the fashion trends.

French Beret

I dreamt of going to Paris France one day, to see hats and fashions as I strolled down the Champs-Elysees.

History:

The Basque beret design became popular in France, worn by both men and women. This soft, lightweight, circular shaped flat, brimless hat is usually made with felt or wool with a stem on the top center.

Berets have been traced back to the Pyrenees Mountains located in southwest Europe in France, which separates France from Spain. The origin of the "Basque" beret is from the Aragonese and Navarrian Shepherds from the Anso and Roncal valleys of Pyrenees.

The Basque-style beret was created in the 17th century. In 1840, the first factory called Beatex Laulhere began production, and many others followed. The beret started out as a knitted hat and was further developed through the process of felting the wool, as well as the addition of water resistance. In the late 1800s, the French Chasseurs Alpins (elite mountain infantry or the French Army) adopted military berets, later other military and activist groups followed.

The beret was associated with the working class and fisherman. During the 1920s, the beret became fashionable by men and women and is still popular today.

Fedoras

Flipping the brim and tilting the hat to the side, while wearing a fedora oh my!

History:
In 1882, the first production of a play called "Fédora," written by French author Victorien Sardou for the actress Sarah Bernhardt in her title role as Princess Fédora Ramanoff popularized the hat. The fedora also became a favorite of Women's Rights activists.

Around 1924, Prince Edward of Britain started wearing the Fédora, and other men soon followed. These hats were made out of felt, with a narrow or wide brim, tapered and pinched on the sides, and contained a center dent or a tea drop center crown finished off with a grosgrain ribbon. The Fedora is sometimes called brim down hat or bent down.

Similar Style Hats:
In the 1600s, the popular Panama hat (aka the Ecuadorian or Toquilla straw hat) originated in Ecuador. This tightly woven hat made from the plaited leaves of the Carludovica palmate plant (palm like plant), is designed as a lightweight, cool and breathable hat made in light-colors.

The Trilby's hat name derives from the novel/play "Trilby" by George du Mauier's in 1894 (preformed in London). This hat has a narrow brim, angled downward at the front and is slightly turned up in the back.

The Tyrolean/Bavarian hat or the Alpine hat originating from the Tyrol in the Alps. Made most popular in Austria, Germany, Italy and Switzerland.

Fascinators

As I wear my Fun Fascinator Hat, people always have something to say, I keep my head up proudly and walk away. "Inspiration Always Stands Out!"

History:
The Fascinator (cocktail hat) has been traced back to the late Renaissance era 16th century. It is a small lightweight headpiece fashionably styled and is usually attached to the head with a headband or hair-clip. Fascinators are usually worn on either side of the head sometimes towards the front.

Netting fabric is also referred to as tulle and or mesh when knitted. The texture is usually stiff, lightweight and made with polyester, silk, nylon and rayon fibers.

Birdcage Veil is usually made with decorated netting styled to cover the head and part of the face and attached to the hair with a comb.

Halo Hat
(aureole, a synonym for halo)
The halo hat is a circular or semi-circular shaped hat. It became fashionable in the late 1880s.

The Halo Brim hat or Aureole Hat is a circular style hat around the face. It has an upturned brim around the head creating a halo effect that is offered in a range of sizes. Halos were a sunrise over anthropomorphic images of the Roman Sun God Helios. A halo is usually shown (in artwork or pictures) above the head of a person in the early days of Christianity, medieval times and during the Renaissance. During the 1930s, it became popular again under the name "aureole-brimmed or aureole hat" and was named Halo during the 20th century.

Sports

There are many hats worn by athletes today and throughout time. Thanks for the discipline, dedication and hard work in order to entertain us all through good times and bad.

History: Baseball Cap

The Brooklyn Excelsior's, an amateur baseball team was formed in 1854. They first wore the "Brooklyn style" cap in 1860, now known today as the baseball cap. These caps were first made with straw and later changed to flannel/wool and other fabrics.

The baseball cap is fitted on the crown of the head (in early days, only one size was offered). An adjustable strap for sizing was introduced in the early 1970s. On the back of the head the cap often displays a team logo, with or without a design. The cap design usually contains 6 panels with metal grommets or fabric eyelets sewn on the top of the crown on each panel for ventilation, a covered button (squatchee) on the crown and a paperboard (later changed to buckram) covered with fabric bib visor (also called bill) to cover the face. Buckram is made of a stiff cotton and stiff linen or stiffened horsehair. Today, it is soaked in pyroxylin to fill all gaps between the fibers for firmness and strength. In 1940, the visor/bill was changed to latex rubber.

In the 21st century, baseball caps were designed with many fabrics and are used well beyond sports team loyalty as a means of functionality, sun protection, comfort, and style.

African American History:

In 1885, the Cuban Giants were the first formed black independent baseball team. Rube Foster, aka "the father of black baseball," founded the Negro National League in 1920. Ed Bolden formed the Eastern Colored League in 1923.

The first recorded history of Hockey occurred in Nova Scotia, Canada by African American slaves who migrated to Canada escaping slavery through the "Underground Rail Road." These black men revolutionized the game.

The Colored Hockey League "CHL" was organized after the last slave reached Nova Scotia in 1895.

A salute to all of the Negro Sports Leagues and athletes who were unable to participate in the major leagues. You will never be forgotten.

Football | Baseball/Softball | Fencing | Racing | Boxing | Skateboarding | Canoeing | Hockey | Equestrian

Golf |Swimming | Golf | Tennis | Snowboarding | Skiing | Bobsleig | Skating | Shooting | Car Racing | Luge

Military and First Responders

Throughout time, the many branches of the military have displayed a variety of hat styles. A salute to the branches of the United States Military and First Responders for their bravery and dedication. Thank you for your service to our country.

Terms

A.D. or a.d. - "In the year of the Lord"

B.C. or b.c. - Before Christ (indicating dates) place after date

Antiquity - Ancient times, before the Middle Ages BCE

Century - A one hundred year period

Crown of the head can mean the whole head or just the top (see how to measure below)

Embroider - Ornament with needlework

Gutter Crown - A dent down the center of the hat crown

Hat - This is a head covering worn for various reasons (style, warmth, safety, sports, religion and more)

Forged - Formed by heating and hammering in a shape

Middle Ages - 500 A.D. to 1350 (sometimes extended to 1450 to 1500)

Milliner - A person who makes and creates hats

Millinery - A hat shop

Trim - Decorations to embellish details

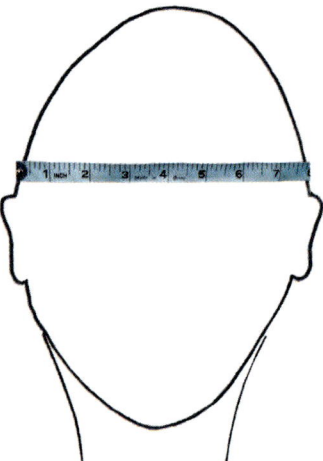

* Measure the circumference of the head above the ears (not tight) to determine the hat size.

Thank You

Writing this book and learning about the traditions and backgrounds behind certain hats and headdresses, has been a spiritual and insightful journey for me. My desire is that this book will allow people to open their minds to embrace and accept differences: cultures and traditions that make us all uniquely special.

I truly hope that you enjoyed reading this multi-cultural book written for all ages as much as I did writing and illustrating it. A special thank you to Felicia Webb-Brown for inviting me to my first polo match in New Jersey (2017) and taking my picture (not knowing that it would capture the full essence of my book).

"Having Faith and Patience God Will Always See Things Through!"

Bibliography

Holy Bible, The New King James Version. Thomas Nelson Publishers, 1979.

Blakemore, Erin. Born into slavery, this man won the Kentucky Derby three times and became the richest American athlete Despite his success, the sport Isaac Burns Murphy helped build disappeared from beneath him as white men pushed black jockeys out. 8 May 2018. Medium. n.d. Jan. 2019 <Web>.

Brockell, Gillian. Jackie Kennedy's fairy-tale wedding was a nightmare for her African American dress designer Ann Lowe was snubbed by the future first lady, who described her as 'a colored dressmaker' without naming her. 28 August 2019. The Washington Post. 15 September 2019 <Web>.

Chico, Beverly. Hats and Headwear around the World. Santa Barbara: ABC-CLIO, LLC, 2013.

Churchill, Alexandra. A Decorative Past: The Surprisingly Noble History of the Pom-Pom. 6 Jan, 2015. Meredith Home Group . 2019 <Web>.

City of London. Lock & Company, The Oldest Hat Shop in the World: the archives of J Lock and Company, hatters. 27 Aug. 2019. City of London. n.d. Dec. 2019 <Web>.

Contributors, Wikipedia. Asian conical hat. 10 Feb. 2020. The Free Encyclopedia Wikipedia. 18 Feb. 2020 <Web>.

Contributors, Wikipedia. Beret. n.d. The Free Encyclopedia Wikipedia. 2019 <Web>.

—. Bucket Hat. 13 Oct. 2019. The Free Encyclopedia Wikipedia. 2019 <Web>.

—. Cowboy. 28 July 2019. The Free Encyclopedia Wikipedia. n.d. Sept. 2019 <Web>.

—. James Lock & Co. 8 Dec. 2019. 15 Feb. 2020 <Web>.

—. Pom-pom. 2 Dec. 2019. The Free Encyclopedia Wikipedia. 2019 <Web>.

—. Uskanka. 24 Dec 2019. The Free Encyclopedia Wikipedia. 2019 <Web>.

—. Wikipedia. 2 Nov. 2018. The Free Encyclopedia Wikipedia. 2 Nov. 2018.

Bibliography

ESPN. Black Ice - CHL Colored Hockey League, Nova Scotia. 9 May 2008. Historical book about

    Halafax, Nova Scotia's (CHL) Colored Hockey League circa1895-1925 Espn segment on book

    "Black Ice". <Web>.

Girl Scouts of the United States of America. 2019. Girl Scouts of the United States of America. 2019

    <Web>.

History of Hats. Baseball Cap - History and Types of Baseball Cap. n.d. History of Hats. n.d. June 2019

    <Web>.

—. Sombrero Hat - History and Types of Sombrero Hats. n.d. History of Hats. n.d. May 2019 <Web>.

Inwards, Harry. Straw Hats: Their History And Manufacture (1922). Kessinger Publishing, LLC, 2010.

JayDee. Thirdshift3. 20 July 2016. 18 Jan. 2019 <Web>.

Journeyman Pictures. Why Some Jewish Women Are Rejecting the Headscarf (2010). 13 July 2016.

    Journeyman Pictures. 2019 <Web>.

Junior, Vic Lang'at. A Brief History Of Cowboy Hats. 24 May 2018. Reunion Technology Inc. 8 Feb.

    2019 <Web>.

KARE11. Uncovering the history of church hats. 8 1 2019. KARE11. 6 June 2019.

Klein, Christopher. The Kentucky Derby's Forgotten Black Jockeys. 22 August 2018. A&E Television

    Networks, LLC. . 16 May 2019 <Web>.

Levine, Sara. Why Do Orthodox Jewish Women Wear Wigs (If They Look Better Than Hair)? 19 Jan.

    2019. Sara Levine. 2019 <Web>.

Library of Congress. Omar Ibn Said Collection. n.d. Arican and Middle East Division. 15 April 2019

    <Web>.

lsccyfairlibrary. MLA Citation for a Wikipedia Page. 17 Dec. 2018. 3 Feb. 2020 <Web>.

LTD, Londonest. The World's Oldest Hat Shop | Lock and Co. 21 12 2017. Londonist Ltd. 12 July 2019

    <Web>.

Major, Gerri. "Dean Of American Designer" Frail New Yorker has spent 50 years creating fashions for

    nations top society. n.d. Dec. 1966. Ebony Magazine. n.d. April 2019 <Web>.

Bibliography

McDowell, Colin. Hats Status, Style And Glamor. New York: Rizzoli International Publications, Inc., 1992.

Mdovri. 29 facts about raincoats. 13 Jan 2020. 2020 <Web>.

Mooney, Katherine. How African-Americans disapeared from the Kentucky Derby. 1 May 2019. Florida State University. n.d. June 2019 <Web>.

Morgan, Thad. Was the Real Lone Ranger a Black Man? 31 Aug. 2018. A&E Televison Networks, LLC. 12 Sept. 2019 <Web>.

Original People. Black Ice: African origins of the sport of Hockey. 3 May 2014. n.d. July 2019 <Web>.

Panne, Valerie Vande. Don't make any assumptions about the next headscarf you see. 29 May 2015. Mashable. 25 Jan. 2019 <Web>.

PBS NewsHour. How the autobiography of a Muslim slave is challenging an American narrative. 23 April 2019. PBS NewsHour. 5 June 2019 <Web>.

Project, The Kings. Story of Black Women, Hats & Church CMBC Women's Hattitude Day 2011. 16 Aug. 2011. The Kings Projects. 2019 <Web>.

Scott, Georgia. Headwraps: a global journey. New York: Peter Osnos, 2003.

Starovit, Veronica. The History of Pointed Birthday Hats. 30 Aug. 2017. Leaf Group Ltd. 18 June 2019 <Web>.

Starovoit, Veronica. The History of Pointed Birthday Hats. 30 Aug. 2017. eHow. 2019 <Web>.

Taylor, Erica. Little Known Black History Fact: Church Hats. n.d. The Tom Joyner Morning Show. 28 Jan. 2019 <Web>.

Vatican News. Pope Francis - Easter - Message and "Urbi et Orbi" Blessing 2018-04-01. 1 April 2018.

Vatican News. Aug. 2019 <Web>.

Wikipedia Contributors. Wikipedia The Free Encyclopdia. The Free Encyclopdia Wikipedia. 20 1 2019 <Web>.

Winfrey, Oprah. Hasidic Traditions and Rules of Modesty | Oprah's Next Chapter. 12 Feb. 2012. OWN. 2019 <Web>.

National Humanities Center Resource Toolbox The Making of African American Identity: Vol. I, 1500-1865. "Oh ye Americans": The Autobiography of Omar ibn Said an enslaved Muslim in the United States. 2007<Web>.